PRICING
FOR PROFIT

GREGORY LEWIS

KOGAN
PAGE

First published in 1992

Kogan Page Limited
120 Pentonville Road
London N1 9JN

© Gregory Lewis 1992

British Library Cataloguing in Publication Data

A CIP record for this book is available from the British Library.

ISBN 0-7494-0832-4

Typeset by Books Unlimited (Nottm), Sutton in Ashfield NG17 1AL

Printed and bound in Great Britain by Clays Ltd, St Ives plc

PRICING

FOR PROFIT

Contents

Introduction

Pricing is a subject which many business managers fail to understand fully.

Too many believe that they can undercut their competitors because their overheads are low. So why can't the corner shop compete with the supermarket?

Too many over-estimate the public demand for their product or service as well as the price they are prepared to pay for it.

Not enough recognise that their pricing policy is an essential part of the business plan which must be prepared to prove that the business is capable of earning a living for the owner and the employees and of making a proper return on the money invested in it.

If this money has to be borrowed it has to be repaid with interest and the lenders of the money will need to examine the business plan which is, in many instances, the only security for their loan.

Pricing, therefore, is part of a disciplined approach to the running of any business and it could even be one of the most important parts.

A computer programme can be used to do the actual calculations involved, but it cannot devise the system. This is something which has to be done by those running the business – after considering all the options for designing a system most appropriate to the industry in which it is involved.

It is hoped that this book will provide an understanding of the subject and offer a basis upon which a sound system can be developed.

Glossary

Available hours Hours available for work allowing for holidays and normal stoppages and interruptions.

Break-even level The level of sales at which gross profit equals running costs and the business makes neither a profit nor a loss.

Break-even pricing A pricing formula based on a predetermined break-even level.

Budget A forecast of business revenue, expenditure and operating performance.

Business plan A detailed explanation of sales, marketing, production and financial implications of a business proposal.

Capacity Production or sales achievable when working for all available hours.

Cash flow The surplus or deficiency of receipts over payments.

Capital invested The value of stocks, debtors, cash at bank and fixed assets minus liabilities to trade creditors, bank and lenders.

Charge-out rate The running cost per effective working hour of the business, a department or group of machines or a single machine.

Direct costs Those associated solely with a job and which would not be incurred if the job was not undertaken.

Direct wages Those paid to machine operators engaged in actual production or those directly engaged in serving customers and whose wages can be directly attributed to a particular product.

Effective working hours The estimated or actual hours expected to be worked.

10   Pricing for profit

Efficiency Time actually taken on a job expressed as a percentage of the estimated or calculated time which should have been taken.

Gross profit The difference between selling price and direct cost.

Indirect costs see Running costs.

Indirect wages Those paid to employees who service the direct workers and whose wages cannot be attributed directly to any product.

Marginal business Orders taken at less than the normal price in order to utilise what would otherwise be idle capacity hours.

Market price The competitive price of a product in the market place.

Mark-up The amount added to direct cost to arrive at the selling price of an article.

Mix of sales The proportions by which individual products make up the range of products contained in the total sales.

Normal price The selling price of a product arrived at by the normal procedure for estimating prices.

Overheads Expenses which cannot be attributed to any product. See Running costs.

Payment terms The time allowed for the settlement of invoices and the possible discount allowed for prompt settlement.

Plant utilisation Actual working hours expressed as a percentage of available hours.

Profit The excess of income from sales over the total direct and running costs representing money available for the replacement of equipment, expansion of the business and shareholders' dividends.

Return on capital Profit expressed as a percentage on capital invested.

Running costs Those which arise purely from running the business and which would be incurred whether or not any sales were made.

1. The relationship of pricing to profit

The relationship is perhaps best explained by a simple example.

A shopkeeper who buys a table for £50 and sells it for £100 makes a profit of £50.

That sounds like good business – but has he really made a profit?

What he has made is not a profit, it is a mark-up or what is called a gross profit – the difference between what the table cost him and what he sold it for.

This mark-up or gross profit has to be sufficient to cover his costs before he can say that he has made a real profit.

His weekly costs are as follows:

	£
He rents a shop which costs him	50
He pays a shop assistant	60
He runs a car for the business and the running costs of that are	20
Other expenses such as telephone, postage, insurance and advertising, average out at a cost of	20
Bringing his total costs per week to	£150

So the sale of the table only pays the rent. He must sell a second table to nearly pay his assistant. If he sells three tables he will be able to pay all his costs. To make an income of £100 per week for himself he has to sell five tables each week.

12   Pricing for profit

He calculates his selling price by adding 100 per cent to his buying cost (that is, doubling it) and although that is an acceptable mark-up, he has to sell a table each day.

A business does not make a profit on each article sold. It makes a profit only when sufficient articles have been sold to make the total gross profit from all the sales greater than the running costs of the business.

Don't be fooled by a good mark-up. Think the matter through and discover what the volume of sales has to be in order to break-even – to make the gross profit equal to the running costs.

In this example the break-even volume is five tables per week because this brings the mark-up to £250 which just pays all the costs including the shopkeeper's income of £100.

At this stage all he has done is make a living, not a profit. Profit is the extra money which must be put aside – like savings – for replacing worn out equipment or improving and expanding the business. When the time comes for the shopkeeper to replace his car he will do so out of his profit, if he has enough saved up. Otherwise the money will have to come out of his own pocket. Assuming that the car cost £2600 and lasts for four years, to replace it will require savings or profit of £650 per year which is equivalent to £12.50 per week.

This is the minimum amount of profit he must make. Because he may want to buy a more up-to-date cash register or even refurbish his shop, he must aim to make more profit than £12.50.

Therefore his selling prices should be high enough to provide a gross profit of at least £262.50 per week – the costs of £150 plus his income of £100 plus the minimum profit of £12.50.

If he cannot be sure of selling more than four tables each week he will need to rethink his pricing. On the other hand, he may feel able to sell as many as six per week, whereupon his problems are considerably easier.

Look at these possibilities:

	1	2	3	4	5
	£	£	£	£	£
Selling price	100.00	115.63	100.00	100.00	100.00
Buying price	50.00	50.00	34.37	50.00	50.00
Gross profit	50.00	65.63	65.63	50.00	50.00
Tables sold	5	4	4	4	6
Total gross profit	250.00	262.52	262.52	200.00	300.00
Running costs	150.00	150.00	150.00	90.00	150.00
Own income	100.00	100.00	100.00	97.50	100.00
Total costs	250.00	250.00	250.00	187.50	250.00
Profit	nil	12.52	12.52	12.50	50.00

- Column 1 shows the position when selling at £100, giving a break-even when five tables are sold.
- Column 2 shows that only four can be sold but the price is increased to £115.63, he can make his profit.
- Alternatively, column 3 shows that if customers will not pay more than £100, the profit can be made still if a cheaper buying price can be found.
- Otherwise, as shown in column 4 running costs must be cut which will mean doing without an assistant and taking a cut in income.
- Column 5 shows that if six tables could be sold per week, even at £100 each, there could be a profit of £50, the assistant's job is saved and there would be money with which to expand the business.

Note that the same £50 profit could be made by selling four tables per week at a price of £125 each if the customers could be found at that price.

You can begin to understand the complexity of pricing and its importance in planning a market strategy.

Remember the fundamental principle of all businesses:

	SELLING PRICE
minus	DIRECT COSTS (the buying price)
equals	GROSS PROFIT
	GROSS PROFIT
minus	RUNNING COSTS (the wages and overheads)
equals	PROFIT

14   Pricing for profit

The three vital facts to observe are:

1. Money received from sales has first to pay for the direct costs.
2. The remainder has to pay the running costs.
3. Anything left over is the profit.

In this and subsequent chapters the terms 'direct cost' – which relates directly to a job or product – and 'running cost' – which relates solely to the running of the business – have been used in preference to the terms 'variable costs' and 'fixed costs'. The latter, although possibly more familiar, are not always used with the same significance. Costs, such as power, which are neither wholly fixed nor wholly variable and are called 'semi-variable' may be included in either the fixed or the variable group and it is not unknown for costs which vary with output to be called fixed because they are 'fixed' per unit of output. Such possible confusion is avoided by the definitions of direct and running costs.

Pricing is all about reconciling costs and sales volume with a price which customers will pay so as to provide a living wage for the proprietors, reliable jobs for employees and a profit to finance the future of the business, and – in larger businesses – to pay dividends to the shareholders.

Price is what a willing buyer will pay and a willing seller will receive.
Profit is money for replacement of equipment, expansion of the business and shareholders' dividends.
Price is not just a matter of an estimated cost plus a profit.

More often than not the price of an article is determined by what people perceive to be its value to them. It is not necessarily directly related to its making cost.

This is why some good ideas turn out to be uncommercial – because the cost of making and marketing exceeds what people are willing to pay. The cost of an article, or of the provision of a service, has to be carefully assessed and set against the market price so that a view can be taken as to its likely profitability.

2. Calculation of prices

Few products are unique. Generally, there is a similar product already on the market, or at least, one which people can buy as an adequate alternative.

When deciding upon a price:

- **Do not** simply add what may appear to be a good mark-up to the direct costs. The mark-up, or gross profit, can vary greatly according to the product and nature of the market for it.
- **Do not** base prices blindly on those of competitors. There is no guarantee that prices which suit them will also be suitable to your business.

It is frequently argued that small businesses can cut prices because they have lower overheads – but this is not always the case.

Consider three possible products for a business which has annual running costs of £15,000 and 1500 available working hours each year (see calculation in Chapter 5).

Each unit of product 1 is labour intensive to produce and requires some expenditure on raw materials, resulting in a direct cost per unit of £42. Product 2 is less labour intensive and requires fewer raw materials, giving a direct cost per unit of £16. Product 3 needs very little labour time but requires very expensive raw materials, resulting in a direct cost per unit of £84. They each have a market price of £70, £40 and £100 respectively.

Product 1 has a gross profit of £28 per unit which is 40 per cent of the market price, but the profit of the business would be only £260 for the year if the whole production capacity were devoted to it:

16   Pricing for profit

1	2	3	4	5
Product	Time required to produce each unit	Market Price per unit	Direct costs per unit	Gross profit per unit (col 3 − 4)
	Hours	£	£	£
1	2.75	70	42	28
2	1.25	40	16	24
3	0.25	100	84	16

1	5	6	7	8
Product	Gross profit per unit (col 3 − 4)	Production capacity (1500 ÷ col 2)	Break-even level (1500 ÷ col 5)	Break-even as % of Capacity (col 7 × 100 ÷ col 6)
	£	Units	Units	%
1	28	545	536	98
2	24	1,200	625	52
3	16	6,000	938	15

Assume 1500 possible working hours during the year,
and that manufacture takes 2.75 hours per unit, production
and sales would equal 545 units.
545 units at a gross profit of £28 per unit gives a total gross
profit of £15,260.
£15,260 minus the running costs of £15,000 leaves a profit
of £260.

No room here for undercutting the competition!

Although product 2 has a lower gross profit, more units can be
produced and therefore the annual profit can be much greater.

With 1500 hours available and using 1.25 hours per unit
production and sales can be 1200 units.
1200 units at a gross profit of £24 per unit gives a total
gross profit of £28,800
£28,800 minus the running costs of £15,000 leaves a profit
of £13,800.

Product 3 has an even lower gross profit but if the whole production capacity were devoted to it, sales could be 6000 units.

6000 units at a gross profit of £16 per unit gives a total
gross profit of £96,000.
£96,000 minus the running costs of £15,000 leaves a profit of
£81,000.

In fact, a profit equal to that which could be made on product 2
could be made with sales of only 1800 units of product 3

1800 units at a gross profit of £16 per unit gives a total
gross profit of £28,800.
£28,800 minus the running costs of £15,000 leaves a profit
£13,800.

Sales of 1800 units would involve the business operating at only
30 per cent of its capacity.

Alternatively, of course, it would be possible for the business to
operate profitably by selling product 3 at a lower price than £100
per unit.

Now compare the break-even levels of the three products – that
is to say the level of sales which provides just enough gross profit
to cover the running costs.

The business would have to operate at more than 98 per cent of
its capacity if it relied solely on product 1, more than 52 per cent
if it sold only product 2, but only 15 per cent if it sold only
product 3.

Before deciding upon a selling price four things must be done.

1. Discover the market price of the product by research of the
   market and by reference to competitor's prices for the same
   or similar alternative products.
2. Ascertain also the size of the market and the likely share of
   that market or volume of sales which might realistically be
   achieved.
3. Calculate the cost of buying or making that volume of
   product and of marketing it – the direct costs – and deduct
   this from the market price to find the amount of gross
   profit available.

4. Calculate the break-even level of sales at the market price – that is the volume of sales which must be achieved to avoid making a loss.

Only then can a price be quoted in full knowledge of all the expectations which must come true to make the business profitable.

Market research can be carried out in many ways:

- Most central libraries have reference books and trade survey reports from which a great deal of information can be extracted for a wide range or markets.
- House-to-house surveys can be made; questions can be asked in the street; manufacturers' catalogues can be analysed.

Market research can be exhausting and very time-consuming but it is vital to the making of a sound business plan.

Having decided upon the price to aim for and formed an idea of the size of the market, it is essential to be aware of the gross profit which might be earned. So calculate the direct costs of each product – which may be the cost of purchasing the product from a wholesaler or the cost of buying the raw materials and components needed for its manufacture. Then, deducting the direct costs from the proposed selling price will give you the gross profit, as in column 5 of the table above.

Sometimes it is more convenient to express the gross profit as a percentage of the selling price:

Product	Selling price	Gross profit	Gross profit as percentage of selling price
	£	£	%
1	70	28	40
2	40	24	60
3	100	16	16

Now an assessment can be made as to whether each product is going to be acceptably profitable for the business to sell or to include in its product range. To do this calculate **The break-even level** for each product. This is arrived at by dividing the running cost by the gross profit per unit.

Column 7 of the previous table shows the break-even levels of the three products in terms of the number of units which have to be sold each year.

Alternatively, it can be calculated in terms of the value of annual sales required by using the formula:

Running cost multiplied by 100 and divided by the gross profit percentage.

For Product 1 – £15,000 × 100 = £1,500,000 divided by 40 = £37,500

For Product 2 – £15,000 × 100 = £1,500,000 divided by 60 = £25,000

For Product 3 – £15,000 × 100 = £1,500,000 divided by 16 = £93,750

Notice that these values are the same as the number of units valued at the selling prices:

For Product 1 – 536 units at £70   = £37,520
For Product 2 – 625 units at £40   = £25,000
For Product 3 – 938 units at £100 = £93,800

A retailer can find out what his total sales must be in order to make a profit. If he decides how much profit he requires, he can draw up marketing plans to achieve it. A manufacturer can do the same but he must also make sure that the capacity of his plant and equipment, and of his workforce, is adequate to produce the volume which he needs to sell.

The break-even level can be expressed as a percentage of the production capacity. Not uncommonly a break-even level may be set at 80 per cent of capacity. This, in effect, means that the factory runs from Monday to Thursday to pay the running costs and on Friday it makes the profit. However, when deciding on the percentage, make sure that the capacity available after passing the break-even level is sufficient to provide the required profit. Using the same three products, if the break-even level were to be set at 80 per cent of capacity the gross profit figures would change. The gross profit per unit would be calculated by dividing the running costs (£15,000) by the number of units required to break-even, as shown in the following table. The required selling price can then be arrived at by adding the direct costs to the gross profit.

1	2	3	4	5	6	7
Product	Capacity	Break-even at 80% of capacity	Gross profit required per unit (£15,000 ÷ col 3)	Direct costs per unit	Selling price per unit (col 4 + 5)	Market price per unit
	Units	Units	£	£	£	£
1	545	436	34.40	42.00	76.40	70.00
2	1200	960	15.63	16.00	31.63	40.00
3	6000	4800	3.13	84.00	87.13	100.00

It is clear that product 1 could not be sold at the market price unless a way could be found to reduce the direct costs.

If the objective is to make a profit of £10,000 there would have to be a rethink of the break-even level, this time to 60 per cent, and a revision to the gross profit which would mean increasing prices. Note that the prices for products 2 and 3 would still remain below the market price:

1	2	3	4	5	6	7
Product	Capacity	Break-even at 60% of capacity	Gross profit required per unit (£15,000 ÷ col 3)	Direct costs per unit	Selling price per unit (col 4 + 5)	Profit per year (col 2 _ 3 × col 4)
	Units	Units	£	£	£	£
1	545	327	45.87	42.00	87.87	10,000
2	1200	720	20.83	16.00	36.83	10,000
3	6000	3600	4.17	84.00	88.17	10,000

These calculations seem to confirm that product 1 is unlikely to be acceptable but products 2 and 3 show promise.

Some people may prefer to look at the break-even level in the form of a graph on which gross profit is plotted against sales. This produces a straight line, starting at zero and rising to represent the increase of gross profit with the increase of sales. Then, by introducing a horizontal line at the level of running costs, the break-even level of sales can be read for any given level of gross profit. The actual profit attainable can also be seen because it is the amount by which gross profit exeeds running costs at each level of sales.

The following chart shows the position for product 2.

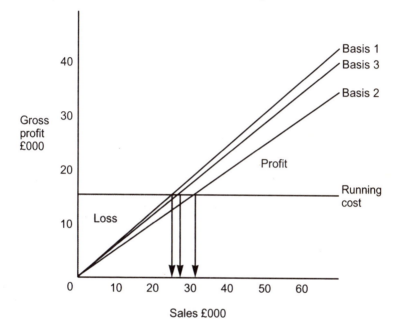

Break-even analysis for product 2

Price	Direct cost	Gross profit	Break-even units	Break-even sales
£	£	£		£

Basis 1 Selling at market price of £70

| 40.00 | 16.00 | 24.00 | 625.000 | 25,000 |

Basis 2 Selling at price required to breakeven with sales at 80% of capacity

| 31.63 | 16.00 | 15.63 | 959.693 | 30,355 |

Basis 3 Selling at price required to break-even with sales at 60% of capacity

| 36.83 | 16.00 | 20.83 | 720.115 | 26,522 |

Gross profit		Break-even		
		Basis 1	*Basis 2*	*Basis 3*
£20,000		833.33 units £33,333	1279.59 units £40,473	960.15 units £35,362
£30,000		1250 units £50,000	1919.39 units £60,710	1440.23 units £53,044

Notice that profit is not earned until sales pass the break-even point. So it is misleading to calculate prices by adding a percentage for profit to the calculated cost of a job or an article in the mistaken belief that each job or article makes a profit. Pricing does not work that way.

Remember:

- Profit is not earned on each sale.
- Profit is earned only when sales in total exceed the break-even level.

From the above examples it can be seen that product 3 has the greatest profit potential and product 1 the least. The marketing strategy should therefore be aimed at securing the maximum sales of product 3. It may be that product 1 should be withdrawn from the range. However, it is often the case that a low profit earner has to be included in order to attract customers for the other products.

As we shall see in Chapter 3, the mix of products within the sales is very important to any multi-product business.

Treatment of VAT in pricing

VAT may be charged by the suppliers of a whole range of goods and services, and unless your business is registered for VAT the amount of VAT included in the cost of your purchases cannot be recovered. For a business which is not VAT registered VAT is a cost and, therefore, when calculating your selling prices, be sure to include any VAT which has been paid on your direct costs and allow for VAT where applicable on your running costs.

If you are not registered you are not allowed to charge VAT on your sales.

A business whose sales exceed an amount prescribed annually by Customs and Excise has to register and this registration changes the situation completely.

A VAT registered business can recover from Customs and Excise all the VAT paid on purchases and must charge VAT to customers if the goods or services sold are defined as *taxable supplies* by Customs and Excise.

So if the business is registered for VAT, remember to exclude the VAT from the cost of your purchases when calculating prices. It is no longer one of your costs because it is recovered. But be sure to add VAT to the prices charged to your customers because you will have to account for VAT to Customs and Excise whether you have remembered to charge it or not.

A VAT-registered customer is interested in the price excluding VAT because it can recover the VAT. So it is not unusual to quote prices excluding VAT; but to avoid any possible misunderstanding, be sure to make clear whether VAT has to be added or not.

Sometimes there may be quite a time gap between quoting a price and receiving an order and it is possible, during this interval, that the government may change the rate of VAT. To be safe some people prefer to quote prices excluding VAT, stating that it has to be added at the rate applicable at the date of sale – the tax-point.

The importance of taking VAT into account in the pricing calculation, whether the business is VAT registered or not, is illustrated by the following example.

1 Capacity Units	*2* Break-even at 80% of capacity Units	*3* Gross profit required (per unit)	*4* Direct costs (per unit)	*5* Selling price excluding VAT (per unit)	*6* Price with VAT (per unit)
		£	£	£	£
Example A – Assuming the business to be VAT registered					
		(£15,000 ÷ col 2)		(col 4 + col 5)	(col 6 + VAT %)
1,200	960	15.63	16.00	31.63	37.17
Example B – Assuming the business is *not* registered for VAT					
		(£16,500 including VAT ÷ col 3)	(including VAT)		(VAT not chargeable)
1,200	960	17.19	18.80	35.99	35.99

Notice that an unregistered business may be able to sell at the lower price of £35.99 compared with £37.17 for a registered business. This may attract an unregistered buyer, but if the customer is registered it can buy effectively at £31.63 from a VAT registered supplier.

For an unregistered supplier to sell at £31.63, its gross profit would be only £12.83 – £31.63 minus £18.80 – and to break even sales would need to be 1286 units which is just above capacity.

Sometimes, especially if most customers are VAT registered, this situation can be avoided if the business registers voluntarily when the level of sales is below the limit for compulsory registration (currently £36,600 per annum (1992–3)).

Taxation

When assessing prices and profits some consideration must be given to taxation because it is the net profit after tax that is of importance to the prosperity of the business.

Tax is payable on the profits of the business which are assessed under rules laid down by the government under which some expenses normally included in a profit and loss account may be disallowed for tax purposes.

The basis of assessment differs for sole traders, partnerships and limited companies. Companies pay corporation tax on profits arrived at after deducting the salaries and fees of directors who are regarded as employees and who are assessed personally for income tax under the PAYE rules. They also have to deduct income tax at the standard rate from dividends paid to shareholders.

Small businesses, currently defined as those earning a profit of less than £250,000, pay tax at a lower rate (currently 25 per cent) instead of the main rate (currently 33 per cent).

Sole traders and partners are not assessed under PAYE and thus their drawings are not taxed. They pay income tax on the profit of their business which is regarded as their personal income. The profit is calculated without deducting drawings. Being personal income, standard personal allowances are deducted from the profit, or their share of the profit in the case of partners, before calculating the amount of tax payable.

So there are various 'break points' to look out for when setting profit targets with tax planning in mind.

Companies should be aware of the cost of tax if profits exceed the small companies' limit of £250,000.

Sole traders and partners should be aware of the level of their personal allowances which will determine the point at which tax becomes payable at the standard rate and of the bands for higher rates of tax.

In either case, it may be worthwhile to assess the benefits of capital expenditure which will increase the capital allowances to be deducted from the profit and to assess the timing of some income or special expenses in order to reduce or perhaps defer the burden of tax.

However, while tax planning is obviously important, it should not be allowed to divert a business from a sound commercial programme or to lead it into an uncommercial one.

3. Mix of products within total sales

Few businesses, in reality, rely on one product. There is usually a range of products or product qualities even if the basic article is the same:

- A joiner makes several types of tables.
- A car manufacturer makes several models.
- A carpet weaver makes many different qualities.

Usually each product within a range yields a different gross profit. Certainly, in a multiproduct business like a retail shop, or like a builder, each article sold or each job undertaken will yield a different gross profit. Obviously, a retail shop or a supermarket sells a very wide range of items.

A marketing plan has to be drawn up to ensure that the sales of a mix of products earn enough gross profit to recover the running costs and leave the required profit.

Assume the running costs to be £15,000 and the profit requirement to be £10,000.

Example 1 shows the result of selling equal quantities of the three products. There is a profit but it does not reach the £10,000 objective.

1	2	3	4	5	6
		Time required for production	Gross profit per unit	Total gross profit	Profit (col 5 minus £15,000)
Product	Number of units sold	(Hours)	£	£	£
1	350	962.5	28	9,800	
2	350	437.5	24	8,400	
3	350	87.5	16	5,600	
	1050	1487.5		23,800	8,800

(Average gross profit per unit = £22.67)

It has already been seen that product 1 is less profitable than the other two products. So see what happens if sales of products 2 and 3 are increased at the expense of product 1.

Example 2 shows the profit objective can be met.

1	2	3	4	5	6
		Time required for production	Gross profit per unit	Total gross profit	Profit (col 5 minus £15,000)
Product	Number of units sold	(Hours)	£	£	£
1	300	825.00	28	8,400	
2	375	468.75	24	9,000	
3	475	118.75	16	7,600	
	1150	1,412.50		25,000	10,000

(Average gross profit per unit = £21.74)

Example 3 shows how the profit could be improved by further reducing the sales of product 1 and increasing those of products 2 and 3.

1	2	3	4	5	6
		Time required for production	Gross profit per	Total gross	Profit (col 5 minus £15,000)
Product	Number of units sold	*(Hours)*	unit £	profit £	£
1	200	550.00	28	5,600	
2	500	625.00	24	12,000	
3	775	193.75	16	12,400	
	1,475	1368.75		30,000	15,000

(Average gross profit per unit = £20.34)

It is interesting to notice that the best profit result – example 3 – is achieved in fewer working hours and with the lowest average gross profit per unit of the three examples.

The most important factor is the total gross profit generated – not the gross profit per unit. The best total gross profit obviously results from getting the right mix of products in the sales.

To achieve maximum profit it is essential to sell the right mix of products.

So far consideration has been concentrated on pricing for retailers and manufacturers of competitive products. The situation can be very different for those who give a service, like builders, interior designers and decorators.

Such businesses are involved in 'one-off' jobs or contracts for which quotations, tenders, or estimates have to be submitted.

It is sometimes very difficult to judge the market price of a product – what people will be prepared to pay for it – especially when a new product or a new design is involved. A very shrewd judgement is often called for to pitch the price at the right level.

The calculation of prices in these circumstances is dealt with in the following chapter.

4. Pricing special products and contracts

If the product to be manufactured has no direct competitor or is of unique design it is necessary to prepare an individual costing in order to arrive at a price.

In the service industries each job, assignment or contract usually has its own individuality.

There is no market price, as such, for decorating a room. The price depends upon the size of the room, which may be small or enormous, and the nature of the job which may involve a large or a small amount of interior designing.

Each job or product has to be costed and priced on its own merits but the underlying principles of pricing still apply.

The price for the job has to be calculated in much the same way as for any manufactured product.

1. Calculate the direct costs.
2. Add an amount for running costs.
3. Add an amount for profit.
4. Compare the result with other similar jobs and make a judgement as to what prices might be quoted by competitors who may have been invited to tender.

Unless the quotation is being made in response to a specification supplied by the purchaser it is wise to attach your own specification. Thus the purchaser is in no doubt as to the nature and quality of the work being suggested. It should ensure that the quotation is compared on a like-for-like basis with others being submitted.

A price consists of three elements, namely:

1. Direct costs - quite easy to define and cost.
2. Running costs - here there are problems. You can run into difficulties when assessing how much of some costs are chargeable to a particular job or product. For example, how much should be allowed for general overheads such as office rent, insurance of plant or the income of the proprietor who may be involved in several jobs at the same time?
3. The inclusion of a profit figure can also be problematical. It can be influenced by the state of trade at the moment or the desperation with which the job is needed.

Now for a closer look at these three elements.

Direct costs

These are the costs associated solely with the job and which would not be incurred if the job was not undertaken.

They will obviously include:

Goods bought for re-sale.
Raw materials to be used in making a product or component.
Components bought specially for the job.
Charges payable to sub-contractors.
Costs of delivery or distribution.
Commission payable to a selling agent.
Wages paid to piece-work employees.
Wages paid to temporary employees taken on specially for the job.

Note that the wages paid to permanent employees not on piece-work would not normally be included because their job is not dependent on the product. They are more likely to be classed as running costs and included in a charge-out rate as explained in Chapter 5. Direct costs can usually be calculated precisely because you are dealing with things that are easily measured. It is not difficult to quantify the material required to make a table or paper a room of a known size after making allowance for both waste and spoilage. For more complex jobs a 'bill of materials' should be prepared, to set out, in detail, all the materials needed and to make drawings to work from if these are not supplied by the purchaser. It should include bought-in parts and components and sub-contract work as well as materials to be used by the business.

A bill of materials can be useful when placing orders and when comparing actual costs with the estimate should the job be obtained.

Running Costs

Sometimes called indirect costs or overheads, these are the costs which arise purely from running the business and would be incurred whether or not any particular product or job were undertaken, or for that matter any work at all.

Such costs would obviously include:

(a) Wages (except those included as direct costs)
   Direct wages – paid to those engaged directly in production
          or selling directly to customers
   Indirect wages – paid to those servicing the direct workers.
   Salaries – paid to office staff and supervisors.

(b) Overheads
   Rent of office or workshop
   Gas, electricity and water
   General insurance of building and plant
   Professional insurance
   Telephones
   Office stationery
   Motor vehicle tax, insurance and running costs
   Depreciation of buildings, plant etc.
   Salaries of directors
   Drawings of the proprietor and partners

Note that some costs are borderline – part direct costs and part running costs.

For example:

- Advertising is a direct cost if it relates specifically to the promotion of a project but it is a running cost if it is general advertising for the business as a whole.
- Loan interest can be a direct cost if the loan is raised especially to fund the project.
- In some instances, such as where the introduction of the product causes shift working to be undertaken, part of the cost of electrical power and heating may be classed as a direct cost and, perhaps, the differential paid for shift work.
- Likewise there are occasions when some additional costs are anticipated in connection with travelling or entertaining which will need to be treated as direct costs.
  Generally speaking, however, these will be classed as running costs.

It may be mentioned at this point that, in the case of a limited company, the salaries and fees of directors are running costs in just the same way as the salaries of other employees.

In the case of a sole trader or a partnership, although the drawings of the proprietor or partners, in accountancy terms, are part of the profit and not part of the costs, it is advisable to include them as running costs when assessing costs for pricing purposes.

There are many ways of charging running costs or overheads to jobs or products and it can be said that none of them is right. After all, one is dealing with expenses which, by definition, have no specific relationship to any one job but relate to the business as a whole.

The traditional alternatives are to use:

1. A percentage of direct cost.
2. A percentage of the wages cost.
3. A percentage of the combined cost of wages and direct costs.
4. A 'charge-out' rate per hour applied to the estimate of time, or man-hours, required to do the job.
5. A range of 'charge-out' rates for each operation, or each trade involved, applied to the estimated time or man-hours involved by them.

You need to form a view as to what generates each of the running costs.

Wages can be divided into 'direct wages' – the people who actually produce things – and 'indirect wages' – those who service the 'directs' like supervisors, salesmen and clerks. The direct wages can be identified with trades or operations. With each trade or operation there are associated costs such as the depreciation of the equipment which they use, the insurance of such equipment, the rent of the work-space they occupy etc. In this way the cost or charge-out rates per hour can be built up for each operation.

The cost of maintaining a warehouse for the storage of raw materials awaiting use in production or on a job could be calculated and expressed as a percentage of the value of the material handled.

A warehouse for the storage of goods awaiting delivery could be costed as a percentage of the value of goods handled or as a cost per square metre to be applied to goods according to the area which they occupy.

It may be argued that the main generators of overheads are stocks and people. Stocks are an investment which costs money which has to be borrowed at a rate of interest, and they take up space which has to be rented. People use telephones, do paper work, travel and entertain clients. It could be said, therefore, that running costs should be applied as a percentage of direct cost plus direct wages.

In the simplest situation you can divide the estimated annual overhead or running cost by the number of working hours in the year which gives you a cost per working hour to be applied to every job or product according to the time each takes. While it may be appropriate for a business employing just two or three people, a more sophisticated system is required for larger concerns.

A cautioning factor is that the more complicated the system is, the more clerical work it creates, or more complex computer programmes have to be written. And remember, the answer can never be accurate.

The essence is to arrive at a system which produces consistently competitive prices, wins orders and leads the business into profit. It is the final order book and the final profit which tell whether the running costs have been properly charged out in the prices.

Profit

This is not required only to provide a dividend for shareholders or a return on the proprietor's capital. It is essentially to fund the replacement of or additions to assets such as equipment and motor vehicles and to provide funds for the expansion of the business. The expansion, or growth, of a business is always very expensive.

Curiously, growth is often the cause of a business failure. Growth means more sales and probably more customers. There is an increase in debtors – people owing money to the business. Trading may be on the basis of payment in 30 days but most customers will nevertheless take 40 days and some as much as 90 days to pay. Throughout this time the business has to pay its own suppliers and its wages bill, both of which have probably increased because of the growth. To pay these increased costs extra funds have to be available and if they are not provided by profit accumulated from previous trading they have to be borrowed – from the shareholders, the proprietor, the partners, the bank or some other source. Borrowing in these conditions is not easy. Who wants to lend to a business which is not making a profit? After all, it is only out of the profit that a lender will be repaid. This shows how much profit is required.

The capital invested in the business is its cash at bank, money owed to it and the value of its property and stocks. This amount of money, if not invested in the business, could have been put into a bank deposit account or a building society to earn interest. In this way it could have provided an income and possibly capital growth without taking any of the risks involved by going into business.

So the profit as a percentage of the capital invested in the business should be at least as great as the percentage available from other types of investment. It should in fact be significantly greater to reward the extra risks taken. This sort of evaluation, known as 'return on capital', is equally important when trying to borrow fresh capital because it allows the potential investor to compare the business with other forms of investment options open to him.

Notice that no mention has been made of the expression of profit as a percentage of sales (sometimes called 'turnover'). Although it is a commonly quoted statistic it is not really very meaningful on its own. It does have a use, however, when linked with the expression of sales as a percentage of capital invested.

It used to be said that a good position was achieved when capital was 'turned over' twice and profit was 10 per cent of sales. 'Capital turned over twice' means that sales are two times the capital invested.

So the situation would be thus:

```
                       £
Capital invested  10,000
Turnover (Sales)  20,000   – twice the capital
Profit             2,000   – 10% of sales and 20% on capital
```

There is one way of putting this relationship to good use. Knowing the capital invested and therefore the profit required, you can calculate the percentage of profit required on any given value of sales.

Alternatively, without ignoring the aspect of return on capital, you can assess the amount needed to fund expansion or some particular objective – which may even be as fundamental as giving the staff a rise in salary.

Having decided what profit needs to be earned the problem is to decide how to include a profit element in the price. As with running costs there are many ways of doing this and none of them is the right way. It is a matter of finding a formula which is most likely to lead to the achievement of the overall profit objective of the business whilst preserving competitive individual prices.

Here are some of the traditional ways:

1. A percentage on total cost – direct cost plus running cost.

2. A percentage on direct cost only.
3. A percentage on running cost only.
4. Include the required profit with the running costs and thus absorb it in the charge-out rate.
5. A fixed rate per unit.

The first of these is equivalent to a percentage on the turnover and makes the profit achievable dependent upon the value of sales. It also means that the more expensive jobs or products contain the greater profit margins which, of course, makes them even more expensive. This is not always desirable.

The use of a percentage on direct cost loads a greater profit margin on to those jobs or products which use or contain the most materials. This is not unreasonable when there is a high cost of financing stocks or forward purchasing of material but it can cause a problem by creating wide differentials when quoting alternatives. The price varies disproportionately with changes in raw material prices.

Applying a percentage only to running costs overcomes this but it ignores the financing costs of stocks. However, it is sometimes thought to be more relevant to achieving a proper return on capital since it does relate profit to time, wages and overhead investment. Including profit in the charge-out rate has the effect of relating it entirely to time but it can be appropriate in industries which are labour intensive: that is, when wages are a very high proportion of the running costs.

A fixed rate per unit could be acceptable in, say, a textile industry, where the profit could be included at an amount per square metre of cloth, irrespective of design. The total profit would then depend solely on the number of square metres sold. The essence is to arrive at a system which produces consistently competitive prices, wins orders and leads the business into profit.

Break-even pricing

Mention has previously been made of this method whereby prices are assessed by determining the operating level at which the business should break-even in order to reach its profit objective.

This method does require that the capacity of the business is known. In the case of a manufacturer capacity is the quantity of product which can be produced in normal hours at an achievable efficiency rate.

For a contractor capacity is the number of working hours or days available.

Suppose the manufacturing capacity is 6000 units and the break-even level is set at 60 per cent of capacity. The break-even level is thus 3600 units. If the running costs are £15,000:

> The gross profit has to be £15,000 divided by 3600 = £4.17 per unit.
> Add £4.17 to the direct cost to give the selling price per unit.

Suppose the time available for contract work is 200 days and the break-even level is set at 60 per cent of capacity. The break-even level is thus 120 days. If the running costs are £15,000:

> The gross profit has to be £15,000 divided by 120 = £125 per day
> Add £125 per day to the direct cost to give the selling price of the job.

Two advantages of the break-even method are its simplicity and the fact that it provides a simple control factor. In the above examples, the manufacturer will make a profit if his sales exceed 3600 units and the contractor if he sells more than 120 days of work.

Clearly it is vital that direct costs be comprehensively calculated and include all costs which will be involved in addition to the running costs.

We return to our example of three possible products first used in Chapter 2.

The illustrations overleaf show prices calculated by four different methods.

The calculated price for product 1 is approximately the same when using the first three methods but greater when using method 4. By each method the price works out higher than the market price of £70.

The result for product 2 is similar except that in each case the calculated price is below the market price of £40.

With product 3, which has a high direct cost and takes only 15 minutes to make, the prices vary considerably with each method, but they all work out at or below the market price of £100.

It would seem that products 2 and 3 are profitable but product 1 would not be very good, unless a way could be found to reduce the direct costs and/or to make it in less than 2.75 hours.

Here you can see how the pricing formula helps in the process of negotiating prices because it shows what has to be done to make a market price acceptable.

Choose the method which gives the most suitable overall result and stick to it.

When a mix of products is sold one must adopt a single method of calculating prices and apply it consistently to all items. Otherwise the ability to judge which are the most profitable products or jobs will be lost.

Finally, make sure that the bookkeeping system is able to present regular information, preferably monthly, on direct costs and the current level of running costs.

There must be very close harmony between bookkeeping and pricing policy in order to achieve good financial control. This means preparing regular statements of income and expenditure, full analysis of expenses and keeping up-to-date budgets and forecasts.

Calculation of prices

Running costs are charged at a charge-out rate of £10 per hour, which is based on costs of £15,000 divided by the 1500 available factory operating hours. Profit is then added using the four alternative methods shown below.

Method 1

We assume the factory is operating at full capacity. The profit element per unit is calculated at 11.11 per cent of total costs per unit, which is equivalent to 10 per cent of the final selling price.

Product	Direct cost (£/Unit)	Running cost (£/Unit)	Total costs (£/Unit)	Profit @ 11.11% of total costs (£/Unit)	Calculated price (£/Unit)
1	42.00	27.50	69.50	7.72	77.22
2	16.00	12.50	28.50	3.17	31.67
3	84.00	2.50	86.50	9.61	96.11

From the information in the above table we can calculate the profit we can expect at full capacity and at 80 per cent of capacity.

At full capacity:

Product	Sales/ Production (Units)	Total costs £	Total revenue £	Profit at full capacity £
1	545	37,877	42,085	4,208
2	1,200	34,200	38,000	3,800
3	6,000	519,000	576,660	57,660

At 80 per cent of capacity:

1	2	3	4	5	6	7
Product	Sales/ Production (Units)	Direct costs (× col 2) £	Running costs £	Total costs £	Revenue (calculated price × sales) £	Profit at 80% of capacity £
1	436	18,312	15,000	33,312	33,668	356
2	960	15,360	15,000	30,360	30,403	43
3	4,800	403,200	15,000	418,200	461,328	43,128

Method 2

The profit element per unit can be calculated as a percentage of direct costs. Using this method the additional profit percentage will need to be higher than the 10 per cent used in Method 1 because we are basing it on only part of the total costs. It is, nevertheless, an arbitrary figure, so let us choose 16.67 per cent.

Product	Direct cost (£/unit)	Running costs (£/Unit)	Total costs (£/Unit)	Profit @ 16.67% of direct costs (£/Units)	Calculated price (£/Unit)
1	42.00	27.50	69.50	7.00	76.50
2	16.00	12.50	28.50	2.67	31.17
3	84.00	2.50	86.50	14.00	100.50

As with Method 1, we can use the information from this table to calculate the profit we can expect at full operating capacity, and at 80 per cent of capacity.

At full capacity:

Product	Sales/ Production (Units)	Total costs (from Method 1) £	Total revenue £	Profit at full capacity £
1	545	37,877	41,693	3,816
2	1,200	34,200	37,404	3,204
3	6,000	519,000	603,000	84,000

At 80 per cent capacity:

Product	Sales/ Production (Units)	Total costs (from Method 1) £	Revenues (price × sales) £	Profit (Loss) @80% capacity £
1	436	33,312	33,354	42
2	960	30,360	29,923	(437)
3	4,800	418,200	482,400	64,200

Method 3

The additional profit can be calculated as a percentage of running costs. Since our running costs in this example are a smaller proportion of total costs than direct costs, we would be well advised to make our choice of percentage substantially higher than that used in Method 2. Let us choose, again arbitrarily, 33.33 per cent.

Product	Direct cost (£/Unit)	Running cost (£/Unit)	Profit @ 33.33% of running costs (£/Unit)	Calculated price (£/Unit)
1	42.00	27.50	9.17	78.67
2	16.00	12.50	4.17	32.67
3	84.00	2.50	0.83	87.33

From the information in the above table we can calculate the profit we can expect at full capacity and at 80 per cent of capacity.

At full capacity:

Product	Sales/ Production (Units)	Total costs (from Method 1) £	Total revenue £	Profit at capacity £
1	545	37,877	42,875	4,998
2	1,200	34,200	39,204	5,004
3	6,000	519,000	523,980	4,980

At 80 per cent capacity:

Product	Sales/ Production (Units)	Total costs (from Method 1) £	Revenue (Price × Sales) £	Profit @ 80% capacity £
1	436	33,312	34,300	988
2	960	30,360	31,363	1,003
3	4,800	418,200	419,184	984

Method 4

As shown in Chapter it is possible to choose a level of output at which we would like to break even, and then to calculate a price which guarantees that we will break even at this level of output. Let us say that we would like to break even at 60 per cent of output.

Product	Sales/ Production @ 60% capacity (Units)	Running costs £	Required gross profit per unit £	Direct costs (£/Unit)	Calculated price (£/Unit)
1	327	15,000	45.87	42.00	87.87
2	720	15,000	20.83	16.00	36.83
3	3,600	15,000	4.17	84.00	88.17

At full capacity:

Product	Sales/ Production (Units)	Total costs (from Method 1) £	Total revenue £	Profit at full capacity £
1	545	37,877	47,889	10,012
2	1,200	34,200	44,196	9,996
3	6,000	519,000	529,020	10,020

At 80 per cent capacity:

Product	Sales/ Production (Units)	Total costs (from Method 1) £	Total revenue £	Profit at 80% capacity £
1	436	33,312	38,311	4,999
2	960	30,360	35,357	4,997
3	4,800	418,200	423,216	5,016

5. Charge-out rate

This is the cost of the whole business per hour worked. Or it can be the hourly cost of a department or a single machine or individual within a department.

Mention has already been made of the use of charge-out rates in the calculation of prices but they can also be used to compare operating efficiency between one period of time and another, to compare the cost of alternative methods or to assess the cost benefit of introducing a machine to replace a manual operation.

A charge-out rate is the estimate of annual running costs divided by the number of working hours in the year.

First prepare an annual budget of running costs by listing each expense individually and carefully estimating its current annual cost. Be careful not to overlook any items.

List only those expenses which are static, or virtually static, whatever the level of production or sales (see Chapter 4 for definitions).

Include the wages and salaries paid to employees and directors except those which are classed as direct costs. The personal drawings required by a sole trader or by partners should also be included because they are part of the business costs for this purpose.

Take into account any anticipated increases in costs because the current or immediate future level of costs must be used for the charge-out rate.

The bookkeeping system should provide a good guide to the expenses of the past which can then be updated to the current levels.

Then calculate the number of working hours in the year.

In one year there are 52 weeks or		365 days
But deduct Saturdays and Sundays		104 days
and deduct Bank Holidays:		
New Year's Day	1	
Easter	2	
Spring holiday	1	
August holiday	1	
Christmas	2	
a total of		7 days
then deduct an annual holiday		
excluding Saturday and Sunday		
already deducted	10 days	
Which leaves – for working	244 days	or 48.8 5-day
weeks		

Assume that each working week contains 40 hours. But not all of these hours will actually be spent working for customers. A sole trader will have to spend time selling and seeing to administrative work. In a factory there will be machine stoppages and time may have to be spent making samples or doing trials. Two ten minute tea-breaks each day will take up 5 per cent of the 40 hours.

So the time actually working for customers may not be more than 75 per cent of the week. Thus each working week has only 75 per cent of 40 hours which equals 30 working hours.

48.8 weeks per year × 30 hours per week
= 1464 working hours per year.

To make our caluclations easier we can round this to 1500 working hours per year.

Example

A small engineering works:

1. Rents a workshop at a cost of £7500 per year.
2. Is equipped with plant valued at £30,000 ie:
   3 capstans, 2 centre lathes, 2 milling machines,
   a drill and ancillary plant.

3. Has office equipment & furniture valued at £1500.
4. Has racking and equipment in the stores which is worth £500.
5. Has a 'pick-up' truck which is worth £3,000.

Apart from the proprietor, who is responsible for the buying, the selling and the making out of quotations, there is a staff of ten people ie:

6 machine operators
1 storeman/labourer
1 labourer/driver
1 shop foreman
1 clerk

A recent profit and loss account shows:

	£	
Sales	160,000	100%
Direct costs	64,000	40% of sales
Gross Profit	96,000	60% of sales
Running cost	87,500	
Profit	8,500	

The balance sheet shows the following capital employed:

	£
Stocks – valued at cost	6,000
Debtors	26,500
Cash at bank	5,000
Current assets	37,500
Creditors – including PAYE, VAT, as well as amounts due to suppliers	12,500
Excess of current assets over liabilities	25,000
Fixed Assets – at cost minus amounts written off as depreciation	30,000
Total assets employed	£55,000

Analysis of running costs

Type of expense	Total £	Operations						
		Capstan £	Centre lathe £	Miller £	Drill £	Stores £	General prod'n £	Admin £
Direct wages & NI	39,000	15,600	11,700	8,450	3,250			
Indirect wages & N.I.	17,500					5,000	12,500	
Salaries & N.I.	3,000							3,000
Consumable stores	250						250	
Repairs	750	300	100	250	50			50
Power, light & heat	1,250	400	275	210	75	40		250
Advertising	300							300
Travelling	825							825
Printing & stationery	300							300
Postage & telephones	600							600
Office expenses	75							75
Professional charges	200							200
Vehicle running costs	1,150							1,150
Bank charges	150							150
Rent & rates	7,500	1,725	2,325	1,162	300	863		1,125
Insurance	500	140	120	70	25	120		25
Depreciation	4,150	1,200	1,000	600	200	100		1,050
Proprietor's drawings	10,000							10,000
Overheads	48,500	3,765	3,820	2,292	650	6,123	12,750	19,100
Total running costs	87,500							

Machine costs:	Capstan	Centre lathe	Miller	Drill
Hours of work which the order book is expected to provide	3,600	2,700	1,950	750
Direct wages/hour	4.33	4.33	4.33	4.33
Overhead/hour	1.05	1.41	1.18	0.87
Total Machine/hour	5.38	5.74	5.51	5.20

Service department costs

Stores

$$\frac{6,123 \text{ (stores costs)}}{64,000 \text{ (direct costs}} \times 100 = 9.56\%$$

General production overheads

$$\frac{12,750 \text{ (general production)}}{39,000 \text{ (direct wages)}} \times 100 = 32.69\%$$

Administration

$$\frac{19,100 \text{ (administration)}}{68,400 \text{ (see below)}} \times 100 = 27.92\%$$

87,500 (total running costs) – 19,100 (administration costs)
= 68,400

Calculation of charge-out rates

A charge-out rate can be calculated for each group of machines. The analysis of running costs shows the direct cost per hour of each group and to this can be added the percentage for general production overheads.

	Capstan lathe £	Centre lathe £	Milling machine £	Drill £
Direct wages	4.33	4.33	4.33	4.33
Overheads	1.05	1.41	1.18	0.87
Total machine cost per hour	5.38	5.74	5.51	5.20
Add:				
General production overheads at 32.6 per cent of direct wages	1.42	1.42	1.42	1.42
Machine charge-out/rate per hour	6.80	7.16	6.93	6.62

The two remaining elements of the running costs – stores and administration – bear no direct relationship to the working hours of the machines and will be included separately in the costing.

Example:

Assume that you have to quote a price for a job which will take five hours on the centre lathe, two hours on the miller and one hour on the drill, and that you have calculated the direct costs at £55. You now have to calculate what gross profit to add to this £55 to give the price to be quoted to the customer.

The gross profit will be:

	£
Machine charge-out rate	
5 hours on the centre lathe at £7.16 per hour	35.80
2 hours on the miller at £6.93 per hour	13.86
1 hour on the drill at £6.62 per hour	6.62
8 machine hours in total	56.28
Stores overhead	
9.56 per cent of direct cost of £55	5.26
Running cost – excluding administration	61.54
Administration overhead	
27.92 per cent of running cost of £61.54	17.18
Total running cost	78.72
Add profit at, say, 5 per cent on cost	3.94
Gross profit	82.66

When added to the direct costs of £55 this will give a price of £137.66.

Alternatively, you could adopt the break-even method of pricing. For this you need first to decide on the level of sales at which the business should break even.

1. The profit and loss account shows the running costs at £87,500 per year and the gross profit at 60 per cent of the sales value.
2. Since at the break-even level gross profit must equal running costs, if follows that if £87,500 equals 60 per cent of the sales value, the break-even level of sales must be £145,833.
3. On the schedule 'Analysis of Running Costs', the calculation of the machine hourly costs and the percentage additions for the service departments assumes a total of 9000 machine working hours and sales of £160,000 as shown in the profit and loss account. Proportionately, this indicates that sales could be £213,333 when operating at the full capacity of 12,000 machine hours.

4. So the break-even sales level of £145,833 represents nearly
   70 per cent of machine capacity.
   70 per cent of the capacity of 12,000 machine hours equals
   8400 machine hours.
5. Dividing the total running costs of £87,500 by 8400 hours
   gives a factory charge-out rate of £10.41 per machine hour.

The calculation of the price is simply a matter of multiplying the
total machine hours by the factory charge-out rate and adding
this to the direct costs.

Example

   5 hours on the centre lathe.
   2 hours on the miller.
   1 hour on the drill.
   8 machine hours in total, at £10.41 per hour = £83.33

When added to the direct costs of £55 this will give a price of
£138.33.

The two methods produce almost the same price and you may
ask – why go to the extra trouble of the first method compared
with the simplicity of the second? The choice depends largely on
your style of management.

The first method, with its analysis of costs, provides several targets and yard-sticks such as machine utilisation (the actual number of hours which machines operate) and the level of
departmental costs. Department supervisors can be made aware
of, and be held accountable for, the level of costs under their
control. It can help to instil a discipline and give greater practical
meaning to the pricing structure.

The break-even method requires the monitoring of the total machine hours worked, the gross profit percentage and the level of
running costs.

To get the best of both worlds, most of the advantages of the first
method could be obtained if break-even levels were set for each
group of machines and hourly charge-out rates assessed for each
group instead of for the factory as a whole.

The following table shows how this can be done. In columns 2 to 4 the machine charge-out rates, as previously calculated, are applied to the anticipated working hours to show the total machine cost. Then, in column 5 the service department overheads are added as a percentage on the machine costs:

	£
Stores	6,123
Administration	19,100
Total	25,223

£25,223 is 40.5 per cent of the machine costs of £62,291.

So, each of the figures in column 5 is 40.5 per cent of the adjacent figure in column 4.

Column 4 and column 5 are then added together to give column 6 which shows the total running cost which adds up to £87,514.

The break-even levels for each group of machines are shown in column 7 and these are the percentages of the capacity working hours which each group is expected to achieve.

Column 8 gives the resulting working hours required when these percentages are applied to column 1. Note that it adds up to 8400 hours which is the break-even level.

Finally, divide column 6 (the running costs) by column 8 (the break-even hours) to provide the break-even charge-out rate per hour for each group.

	1	2	3	4	5	6	7	8	9
								Hours to be worked to break even	Break-even rate per hour
	Capacity working hours	Effective working hours	Rate per hour £	Machine cost £	Add stores & admin/ overhead £	Total running cost £	Break-even %		£
Capstan	4,500	3,600	6.80	24,480	9,913	34,393	75	3,375	10.19
Centre lathe	3,000	2,700	7.16	19,332	7,828	27,160	85	2,550	10.65
Miller	3,000	1,950	6.93	13,514	5,472	18,986	60	1,800	10.55
Drill	1,500	750	6.62	4,965	2,010	6,975	45	675	10.33
Totals	12,000	9,000		62,291	25,223	87,514		8,400	

The calculation of a price using these group rates is as follows:

	£
5 hours on the centre lathe at £10.65 per hour	53.25
2 hours on the miller at £10.55 per hour	21.10
1 hour on the drill at £l0.33 per hour	10.33
giving total cost of	84.68

When added to the direct costs of £55 this will give a price of £139.68.

The break-even method using a factory charge-out rate has the great advantage of simplicity for a business under the tight control of the owner. One of the other methods would probably be more suitable and offer better control facilities to a business where management is delegated to department supervisors.

Note at this point that the bookkeeping system should be designed so that it provides regular information on such matters as the current ratio of gross profit to sales, the level of expenditure on running costs and the current value and product mix of the sales.

6. Estimates, quotations and tenders

An estimate is strictly an approximation, an idea, a suggestion as to what an article or job may cost: For example, 'I think this job will cost about £X'.

A quotation is a statement of fact: For example, 'I will do this job for £X'.

A tender is a quotation in a particular format which is normally drawn up by the buyer for the supplier to complete. Attached to it will be detailed drawings and specifications of his requirements.

An estimate, quotation or tender should always be submitted in writing for the avoidance of future doubt.

An estimate is not binding, but there would need to be a good reason or an acceptable explanation for the final charge to differ greatly from the estimate. The buyer will try to hold the supplier to his estimate so, if there is likely to be any deviation, it is wise to point it out as it arises.

An estimate for the decoration of a room presupposes the use of certain materials and presumes no hidden difficulties. Misunderstandings over materials can be avoided by specifying them, or by showing their cost separately, or by excluding them altogether on the basis that they will be supplied by the customer.

As for unforeseen difficulties, there could be a note on the estimate absolving the supplier and allowing an extra charge to be made if any arise.

The estimate can be written out on any plain sheet of paper, or on a specially printed form, but it must be dated and state for how long it is valid.

A quotation or a tender is not binding until it is accepted by both parties – the buyer and the supplier. Then it becomes binding.

Legally, quotations and tenders are offers or invitations, not promises. They can be withdrawn at any time before they are accepted. Even if the buyer accepts, the supplier can still withdraw and is then not bound. But if he also accepts, he becomes bound to do the job for the price stated and the quotation, or tender, becomes a promise.

Quotations must be prepared very carefully and all likely problems must be recognised and taken into account. Any conditions with regard to the price, or the delivery dates, must be stated.For example – unless the quotation states something to the contrary:

- The price cannot be altered if the supplier finds that, because of inflation, or any other reason, his materials cost more than he expected.
- Things like strikes, lock-outs and acts of God cannot be used as reasons for not completing the job, or not completing it on time.

The specification attached to a tender frequently contains some items which cannot be defined in detail. Perhaps it is something to be left to the choice of the buyer at a later date: for example, a bathroom suite in a building contract. Or perhaps it cannot be detailed until it is examined by some third party, eg 'Excavate and expose drains as required by local authority.'

In these circumstances it is usual to quote a provisional cost sum which gives the supplier the right to quote a firm price when all the facts are known. Such provisional cost sums are often inserted by the buyer to give him a notion of the overall cost of the job. They do not really form part of the contract. When details are available he can obtain quotes from other possible suppliers as well as the main contractor.

In other respects the quotation is firm and binding.

Buyers must understand that any variations from the original plan or specification which they request during the carrying out of the job will be treated as 'extras'. They will be priced separately and will be additional to the quoted price.

Big contracts, like building a house, call for the services of many trades. It is customary for the buyer, or his architect, to offer the tender to a main contractor who, in turn, sub-contracts to other tradesmen the work which he himself is not equipped to do.

Sub-contractors will submit their quotes to the main contractor who will combine them with his and submit the full tender to the buyer.

The sub-contractor gets the job only if the main contractor's bid is successful.

Sometimes a sub-contractor will be quoting to several potential main contractors each of whom is bidding for the same contract.

The sub-contractor must be quite clear about the terms of his contract with the main contractor and also the terms under which the main contractor is quoting to the buyer. Some of them may reflect on him, particularly where payment is concerned.

Often the terms of a tender are linked to an industry standard form of contract.

Particular note should be taken of such things as:

- Specification details – standard of workmanship and materials.
- Warranties – liabilities for quality, damage, or delay.
- Commencement and completion dates.
- Penalty clauses – a payment required from the supplier in the event of late completion.
- Terms of payment.

A contractor may specify his own conditions of sale which set out his terms and requirements for payment. It is advisable for all suppliers to draw up their own conditions of sale. To make sure that every aspect is covered have them prepared by a solicitor who is acquainted with commercial practice.

However, while these are a safeguard, in the case of a big contract, it will probably be necessary to come to a compromise between the terms and conditions laid down by the buyer and the seller.

Think carefully about the terms of payment. In a building contract, for example, stage payments may be made monthly when the quantity surveyor has carried out his inspection and given a certificate to the buyer, or the main contractor, advising him of the value of the work done and how much payment should be released to each supplier.

Frequently something like 5 per cent of the quoted price is retained by the buyer for six or twelve months at which time defects have to be rectified before this retention is paid over. Beware of statements in the tender document that stage payments will be made monthly or within so many days of the quantity surveyor's certificate. Such payments have been known to come even ten to twelve weeks later than anticipated.

The supplier must make himself aware of when the quantity surveyor is to carry out his inspection and when site meetings are being held and submit his claim for payment at the right time. Otherwise he might just find himself overlooked until the next inspection.

The financial implications of each of the clauses in the tender must be weighed up carefully and included in the price quoted. It is sometimes said that some contractors intentionally quote a keen price to secure a contract in the belief that there will be extras on which they can make up their profit. This is a dangerous practice.

A supplier's conditions of sale can have greater influence in a manufacturing industry.

A manufacturer may request, for example:

- A deposit of one-third of the quotation to be paid to him when the order is placed.
- One-third to be paid when the product is ready for despatch.
- And the final third within 30 days of despatch.

Such arrangements are common in the engineering industry and others. They certainly should be sought by the manufacturer for any job that extends over a longish period of time. They help cash-flow and perhaps keep the overdraft down.

Obtaining a big contract can give one a feeling of achievement and do the ego a power of good, but do not overlook the cost of financing. It has to be reckoned with.

Consider the cash-flow profile of a business:

1. There is normally a waiting period of some 8 to 10 weeks between the completion and invoicing of an order and the receipt of money from the customer – even if the terms are 'payment in 30 days'.
2. During this time suppliers of raw materials may have to be paid and there will be on-going payments of wages and overhead expenses.
3. In consequence, the business must have sufficient cash resources from which to pay some 90 per cent of the value of the order before any money comes from the customer and a profit is in the bank.

Example

Assume a mix of orders worth £20,000 is produced and invoiced in February on 30-day payment terms.

Materials will have to be paid for in March but assume that just a few customers will pay very promptly and although most will pay in April some will not pay until May or even June.

	Total £	February £	March £	April £	May £	June £
Materials purchased in February & paid for in March	8,500		8,500			
Wages & overheads paid as incurred	10,500	10,500				
Total payments	19,000	10,500	8,500			
Cash received	20,000	NIL	1,000	13,000	5,000	1,000
Monthly Cash-flow		−10,500	−7,500	+13,000	+5,000	+1,000
Cumulative Cash-flow	+1,000	−10,500	−18,000	−5,000	NIL	+1,000

	Total £	February £	March £	April £	May £	June £
Interest at 1% per month on excess of payments over receipts	335	105	180	50		

Notice that interest on the 'overdraft' at £335 absorbs as much as one third of the profit.

Assuming that the business continues at this monthly level of sales, the cash-flow position can be summed up like this.

	Net Cash Received (+) or Spent (−)					
	February £	March £	April £	May £	June £	July £
From trading in						
February	−10,500	−7,500	+13,000	+5,000	+1,000	
March		−10,500	−7,500	+13,000	+5,000	+1,000
April			−10,500	−7,500	+13,000	+5,000
May				−10,500	−7,500	+13,000
June					−10,500	−7,500
July						−10,500
Cash flow						
Monthly	−10,500	−18,000	−5,000	0	+1,000	+1,000
Cumulative	−10,500	−28,500	33,500	−33,500	−32,500	−31,500

Notice that the 'overdraft' rises to £33,500 by the end of the third month and only then will it very slowly reduce.

If there were to be some growth in sales, the 'overdraft' would be greater, but the additional profit which would be generated, would help to reduce it more quickly in the following months.

Curiously enough, if sales were to decline, there could be a temporary drop in the 'overdraft' while the business enjoyed the income from greater sales in earlier months. But very soon the position would worsen as the amount of incoming cash reduced – unless, of course, compensating savings could be made in wages or overheads.

The downfall of many a business – both large and small – has been caused by the failure to recognise the financial profile and make proper provision for the varying demands for working capital.

The tender document

Example of a simple form of tender.

Tender
To: Harold & Smith, Architects, London Road.

Sirs:
I/We hereby offer to execute the work described below for the sum of

....(£   .   p)

I/We further agree that my/our offer is open for acceptance for a period of 90 days from the date fixed for lodgement of this tender.

The work will be let in accordance with the standard form of building contract, a copy of which can be inspected at the architect's office.

Name:
Address:

Signed:
Date:

Extension to house at Curzon Way.

1.	Masonry, brick, concrete & drainage works	£
2.	Joiner & glazier works	£
3.	Plumbing work	£
4.	Plaster work	£
5.	Roofer work	£
6.	Electrical work	£
7.	Painter work	£
8.	Specialist work	£_____
9.	Add 5% contingencies	£_____
	TOTAL	£_____

Each of the sections numbered 1 to 9 of this summary would be supported by a detailed list of work to be done. Each item on each list would be priced and the totals for each section carried forward to the summary.

7. Negotiating prices

When an estimated price is quoted to a customer it is quite possible that he will not accept it.

Returning to our example in chapter 5, the business may quote a price of £87.08 for a job, having calculated direct costs of £35 and added a gross profit of £52.08 being 5 hours of work at £10.41 per hour.

If the customer's response is that he will not pay more than £80 what options are open?

Assuming that the price has been accurately calculated, there are two main options:

1. Can a cheaper source of raw materials be found, without prejudice to quality, to reduce the direct costs from £35 to £27.92 so that adding the gross profit of £52.08 would give a price of £80?
2. Can the job be done in 4.25 hours so that the gross profit at £10.41 per hour would be £44.27 and with direct costs still at £35 the price of £80 would be acceptable?

If either, or some combination of each, of these can be done the price can safely be revised to £80.

If neither of them are possible: check the effect on the break-even analysis.

A price of £80, with direct costs of £35, gives a gross profit of £45. For such a gross profit to be achieved the charge-out rate for 5 hours of work would need to be £9 per hour. In turn, to get a charge-out rate of £9 would require a break-even level of 9722 working hours per year instead of the assumed 8400 hours. To work for 9722 hours of the available 12,000 hours means operating at 81 per cent of capacity whereas the estimated price was based on 70 per cent.

It is not impossible to achieve 81 per cent so the price of £80 could be accepted but it must be recognised that unless 9722 hours are actually worked there may be a drop in profit for the year.

However, the customer should be told that the reduction is for this order only and may not be repeatable.

If the reduction of the quoted price raises the break-even to an impossible level, withdraw and look for another customer.

Nevertheless, the price of £80 gives a gross profit of £45 and does make a contribution to the recovery of the running costs. To this extent it could be better to accept the order. It will provide work for production plant which might otherwise stand idle. It may thereby improve the profit for the year although it will most likely prevent the business from achieving its profit target. Before making a decision, consider carefully such matters as the state of the order book and the likelihood of more profitable business becoming available.

Orders taken at less than the normal price, sometimes called 'marginal business', can boost the profit significantly once sales have exceeded the break-even level, but too much 'marginal business' can make the break-even level so high that it is very difficult to make a profit at all.

A mix of orders, each with a different gross profit ratio, creates a situation rather like that of a mix of products within the total sales which is discussed in Chapter 3. It is necessary to establish a balance between normal and marginal business to ensure that the optimum total gross profit is achieved.

8. Marginal business

When trading is quiet there is a temptation to reduce prices and cut profit margins to get orders.

It is true that any price which exceeds the direct cost of the job or product contributes to the gross profit and improves the overall profit of the business.

But there are constraints:

1. The percentage reduction from any normal price must never be greater than the percentage gross profit which that normal price yields.
2. If sales are currently below the break-even level any price reduction may have to be restrained because until this level is reached even the reduced price orders are part of the core business which has to recover running costs.

Consider, for example, a business having running costs of £87,500 per year and capable of sales of £675,000 with direct costs taking 84 per cent of the value leaving a gross profit of 16 per cent. From sales of £675,000 it would expect the gross profit to be £108,000 and the profit £20,500.

With sales at the rate of £560,000, which is just above the break-even level, the profit could be augmented by marginal sales at a discount of, say 7.5 per cent.

	Sales £	Direct cost (at 84% of normal price) £	Gross profit £	Running cost £	Profit £
Sales at normal prices	560,000	470,400	89,600	87,500	2,100
Marginal sales; £100,000 at 7½% discount	92,500	84,000	8,500	–	8,500
	652,500	554,400	98,100	87,500	10,600

If the marginal sales had been at a discount of 16 per cent they would have produced no additional profit and, of course, if they had been at 20 per cent discount their sales value at £80,000 (£100,000 minus 20 per cent) would have been £4,000 less than the direct costs and the profit of £2,100 would have become a losss of £1,900.

Even with sales at £450,000, well below the break-even level, marginal sales could help to restore a profitable result.

	Sales £	Direct cost (at 84% of normal price) £	Gross profit £	Running cost £	Profit £
Sales at normal prices	450,000	378,000	72,000	87,500	(15,500)
Marginal sales; £200,000 at 5% discount	190,000	168,000	22,000	–	22,000
	640,000	546,000	94,000	87,500	6,500

The position would be quite different if the normal price gave a greater percentage gross profit. Much larger percentage discounts would then be acceptable. Consider a business with the same running costs of £87,500 but the capability for sales of £180,000 at a gross profit of 60 per cent of that value.

From capacity sales of £180,000 the business would expect a profit of £20,500, but if sales were at only half that level – at £90,000, which is well below the break-even level – a profit could still be achieved if the otherwise idle capacity could be sold at a discount of 10 per cent.

	Sales £	Direct cost (at 40% of normal price) £	Gross profit £	Running cost £	Profit £
Sales at normal prices	90,000	36,000	54,000	87,500	(33,500)
Marginal sales; £90,000 at 10% discount	81,000	36,000	45,000	–	45,000
	171,000	72,000	99,000	87,500	11,500

It is quite clear that, before undertaking marginal business, careful thought must be given to the gross profit percentage, which controls the possible level of discount, and the proportion of normal to discounted sales.

The temptation to obtain orders at discounted prices, has always to be balanced against the possibility that better priced business may come along. But a decision has to be made – usually at a time when it is difficult to be sure that the capacity will not be sold, ultimately, at better or even normal prices.

Few businesses can hope to operate at full capacity for every week of the year so it may be wise to make an assumption at the outset that only, say, 80 per cent of capacity will be sold at normal prices. A profit target can then be drawn up on the basis that the remaining 20 per cent is available to marginal business.

The situation can be reviewed in the light of trading conditions but such a plan can be helpful when opportunist decisions have to be made. An example is shown overleaf.

	Sales £	Direct cost (at 40% of normal price) £	Gross profit £	Running cost £	Profit £
Sales at normal prices 80% of capacity	144,000	57,600	86,400	87,500	(1,100)
Marginal sales; £36,000 at an average of 15% discount	30,600	14,400	16,200	–	16,200
	174,600	72,000	102,600	87,500	15,100

This plan suggests that, although the profit could be £20,500 if full capacity could be sold at normal prices, a more realistic profit target would be £15,100.

Another way of expressing the target is that, allowing for holidays, the gross profit must average £2,100 per week. The progress towards achieving this can be checked easily from the bookkeeping records of sales and direct costs.

Adjustments can be made to prices and marketing policy, whenever possible, to keep gross profit and running costs within range of the target.

The regular analysis of gross profit and its relation to running costs is a discipline which must be followed regularly to ensure optimum profit.

Marginal business, therefore, has advantages but it must not be undertaken without most careful thought.

Be aware of the real dangers which must be avoided:

1. Cut prices on some orders can lead to a general price reduction on all orders.
2. Cut prices reduce the gross profit and increase the break-even level.
3. Too much cut-price work can raise the break-even level to a point which makes it impossible for the business to make a profit.

The ultimate aim is to make the total gross profit for the year exceed the running costs.

Price reductions, special offers, annual sales etc, can help to boost the gross profit when they have the effect of selling off what would otherwise be capacity lying idle.

Pricing is a juggling act:

- Be fully aware of what customers want to buy and what they are prepared to pay.
- Match quoted prices to the demand.
- Secure the maximum gross profit.
- Be conscious of the business break-even level.
- Aim for maximum operating efficiency and maximum utilisation of plant.
- Keep running costs under control and make sure that they are less than the amount of the gross profit.

Use a bookkeeping system from which you can constantly monitor, at least:

- Direct costs
- Gross profit
- Running costs

9. Research, design and development

Those who are able to introduce a new or unique product to the market need to keep a special account of all relevant expenditure from the conception of the idea until the first saleable articles are produced.

The cost of market research, the production of prototypes, all the design work and, perhaps, launch promotional advertising and test-marketing programmes, cannot always be included in the price estimates of the direct costs for the first saleable production. Nor should they be included in the running costs in the months in which they are incurred because this would have the effect of increasing the estimated prices of all other products which are probably not related to the new one.

On the basis of the market research it should be possible to assess the likely volume of sales of the product. The research, design and development costs can then be spread over this volume.

Alternatively, it can be spread over a smaller volume so as to 'write off' the costs sooner and present the possibility of a subsequent price reduction to give an extra boost to sales at a later date.

A unique product should command a premium price. Do not give it away. Remember that some extra profit could help to finance the further development of a 'follow-up' invention and keep prices reasonable for its launch.

Example

Assume development costs of £500,000

Sales are projected at 50,000 articles during its five-year life.

	£
Normal estimated price	100
Add: Development costs £500,000 ÷ 50,000	10
Proposed selling price	110

Or:

Spread the development costs over the first 10,000 articles sold.

	£
Normal estimated price	100
Add: Development costs £500,000 ÷ 10,000	50
Proposed selling price	150

This will give some insurance should the projected sales of 50,000 prove to be too optimistic or slow in materialising.

If necessary, sales in excess of the first 10,000 could be reduced in price, by stages, to £100.

Bear in mind that the ultimate price of any article is what a consumer is prepared to pay for it.